Lobsters

by Heather Adamson

BELLWETHER MEDIA • MINNEAPOLIS, MN

BLASTOFF!
READERS
3

Note to Librarians, Teachers, and Parents:

Blastoff! Readers are carefully developed by literacy experts and combine standards-based content with developmentally appropriate text.

Level 1 provides the most support through repetition of high-frequency words, light text, predictable sentence patterns, and strong visual support.

Level 2 offers early readers a bit more challenge through varied simple sentences, increased text load, and less repetition of high-frequency words.

Level 3 advances early-fluent readers toward fluency through increased text and concept load, less reliance on visuals, longer sentences, and more literary language.

Level 4 builds reading stamina by providing more text per page, increased use of punctuation, greater variation in sentence patterns, and increasingly challenging vocabulary.

Level 5 encourages children to move from "learning to read" to "reading to learn" by providing even more text, varied writing styles, and less familiar topics.

Whichever book is right for your reader, Blastoff! Readers are the perfect books to build confidence and encourage a love of reading that will last a lifetime!

This edition first published in 2018 by Bellwether Media, Inc.

No part of this publication may be reproduced in whole or in part without written permission of the publisher. For information regarding permission, write to Bellwether Media, Inc., Attention: Permissions Department, 5357 Penn Avenue South, Minneapolis, MN 55419.

Library of Congress Cataloging-in-Publication Data

Names: Adamson, Heather, 1974- author.
Title: Lobsters / by Heather Adamson.
Description: Minneapolis, MN : Bellwether Media, Inc., 2018. | Series:
   Blastoff! Readers: Ocean Life Up Close | Audience: Age 5-8. | Audience: K
   to grade 3. | Includes bibliographical references and index.
Identifiers: LCCN 2016052736 (print) | LCCN 2017005259 (ebook) | ISBN
   9781626176423 (hardcover : alk. paper) | ISBN 9781681033723 (ebook)
Subjects: LCSH: Lobsters–Juvenile literature.
Classification: LCC QL444.M33 A323 2018 (print) | LCC QL444.M33 (ebook) | DDC
   595.3/84–dc23
LC record available at https://lccn.loc.gov/2016052736

Editor: Christina Leighton   Designer: Lois Stanfield

Printed in the United States of America, North Mankato, MN.

Table of Contents

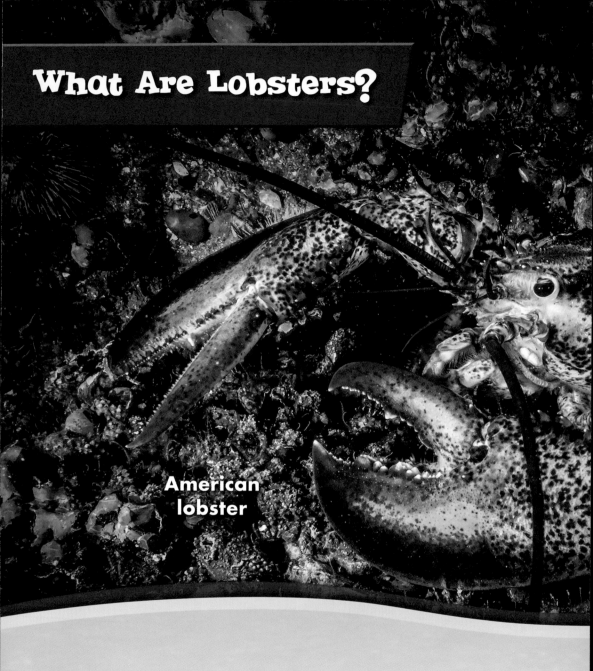

American
lobster

Lobsters are **crustaceans** known for their hard outer shells and long tails.

Other
Crustaceans

barnacles

crabs

shrimp

leg

These animals have ten legs.
They use them to walk on the
bottom of the ocean.

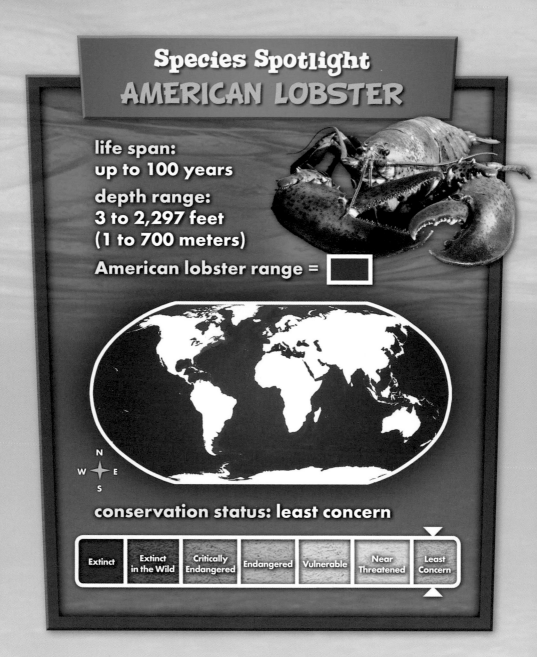

Species Spotlight
AMERICAN LOBSTER

life span:
up to 100 years

depth range:
3 to 2,297 feet
(1 to 700 meters)

American lobster range =

conservation status: least concern

Extinct	Extinct in the Wild	Critically Endangered	Endangered	Vulnerable	Near Threatened	Least Concern

Lobsters are found near the shores of many oceans. They often live in water less than 165 feet (50 meters) deep.

Most lobsters live on rocky or weedy ocean floors. There, they have places to hide.

Sizes and Colors

Lobsters come in many different sizes. Tiny lobsters are only a few inches long.

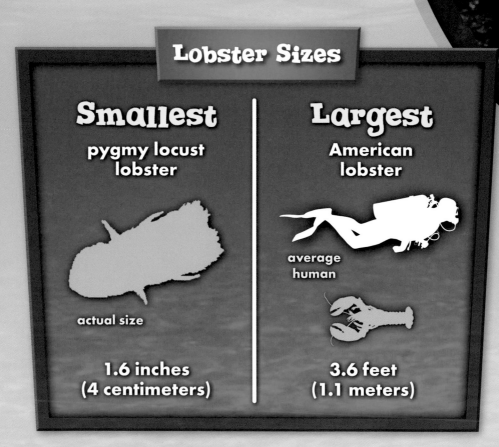

Lobster Sizes

Smallest
pygmy locust lobster

actual size

1.6 inches
(4 centimeters)

Largest
American lobster

average human

3.6 feet
(1.1 meters)

Large lobsters can weigh
more than 40 pounds
(18 kilograms) and measure
over 3 feet (1 meter) long!

Most lobsters are green or brown. These colors **camouflage** them in weeds and rocks.

Mediterranean slipper lobster

Identify a Lobster

antennae

ten legs

long tail

A few kinds of lobsters are yellow or blue. Spiny lobsters can be colorful.

Finding Food

antennae

eyestalk

Lobsters have eyes on the ends of **eyestalks**. However, their eyesight is poor. Two pairs of **antennae** help lobsters find food.

Lobsters use their legs to grab food from the ocean floor.

European lobster

13

Catch of the Day

blue mussels

green algae

long-spined sea urchins

These **omnivores** like to eat mussels, worms, and small fish. They also eat plants.

Some lobsters have big claws. Crusher claws crack shells, and **pincer** claws hold and tear apart **prey**. Other lobsters use strong jaws to crush food.

pincer

crusher

Hiding and Growing

Few animals eat lobsters. These crustaceans hide well. If they are spotted, their hard outer shells help protect them.

Lobsters with big claws use them to scare away **predators**. When in danger, lobsters may use their tails to quickly swim away!

Sea Enemies

Atlantic cod

common octopus

moray eels

Caribbean spiny lobster

Female lobsters carry eggs under their bodies. They hide the eggs until the **larvae** are ready to **hatch**.

Life Cycle of a Lobster

eggs

larvae

adult

young adult

Newborn lobsters are tiny. They float at the surface for a few weeks before sinking to the ocean floor.

molting

Lobsters must **molt** to grow. They break out of their old shells. Lobsters are soft until their new shells harden.

They molt many times in their lives. Each time lobsters molt, they are bigger and stronger!

Glossary

antennae—feelers on a lobster's head that help it touch, smell, and taste

camouflage—to use color in order to blend in with surroundings

crustaceans—animals that have several pairs of legs and hard outer shells; lobsters and crabs are types of crustaceans.

eyestalks—moveable stems that have an eye at each tip

hatch—to break out of an egg

larvae—early, tiny forms of an animal that must go through a big change to become adults

molt—to shed a skin layer or shell so a new one can grow

omnivores—animals that eat both plants and animals

pincer—a sharp, pointed claw

predators—animals that hunt other animals for food

prey—animals that are hunted by other animals for food

To Learn More

AT THE LIBRARY

Magby, Meryl. *Lobsters*. New York, N.Y.: PowerKids Press, 2013.

Pallotta, Jerry. *Lobster vs. Crab*. New York, N.Y.: Scholastic, Inc., 2014.

Pettiford, Rebecca. *Crabs*. Minneapolis, Minn.: Bellwether Media, 2017.

ON THE WEB

Learning more about lobsters is as easy as 1, 2, 3.

1. Go to www.factsurfer.com.

2. Enter "lobsters" into the search box.

3. Click the "Surf" button and you will see a list of related web sites.

With factsurfer.com, finding more information is just a click away.

Index